Phonics Fun
Reading Program Book 7: sm, sn, sl, st, sk

A Day in the Woods

by Donna Taylor

Illustrated by Robin Cuddy

Based on the books by Norman Bridwell

SCHOLASTIC INC.
New York Toronto London Auckland Sydney
Mexico City New Delhi Hong Kong Buenos Aires

Phew! What do they smell?

What stinks?

Sniff! Sniff!

What can it be?

The dogs sniff here.

They sniff there.

They see a beaver.

He wants to cut down the tree.

The dogs dig here.

They dig there.

T-Bone finds a bone.

They dig deep holes.

Hiss! Hiss!

Stop!

Let the little snake
slip away!

Clifford and his pals are in the woods.

The dogs look here.

They look there.

They see a raccoon.

He likes to sleep
under the tree.

Shh! Shh!